50 Breakfast in Bed Recipes for Home

By: Kelly Johnson

Table of Contents

- Fluffy Buttermilk Pancakes
- Croissant Sandwich with Ham and Cheese
- Overnight Oats with Almond Milk
- Mini Quiches with Spinach and Cheese
- French Toast Sticks with Maple Syrup
- Smoothie Bowl with Granola
- Scones with Clotted Cream and Jam
- Avocado Toast with Radish
- Chocolate Chip Banana Bread
- Poached Eggs on Toast
- Yogurt Parfait with Berries
- Breakfast Burrito with Avocado
- Cinnamon Roll Pancakes
- Savory Breakfast Bowl with Quinoa
- Berry Smoothie with Oats
- Omelette with Fresh Herbs
- Breakfast Tacos with Scrambled Eggs
- Granola with Yogurt and Honey
- Sautéed Apples with Cinnamon
- Biscuit and Gravy Casserole
- Chia Seed Pudding with Coconut
- Fruit Salad with Mint
- Egg and Cheese Breakfast Muffin
- Coconut French Toast
- Zucchini Bread with Walnuts
- Lemon Ricotta Pancakes
- Tofu Scramble with Veggies
- Bagel with Cream Cheese and Smoked Salmon
- Raspberry Almond Overnight Oats
- Breakfast Flatbread with Eggs
- Sweet Potato Hash with Eggs
- Porridge with Dried Fruits
- Blueberry Muffins
- Baked Apples with Oats
- Spinach and Feta Breakfast Wrap

- Chocolate Smoothie with Peanut Butter
- Stuffed French Toast with Berries
- Egg Salad on Toast
- Avocado and Egg Breakfast Bowl
- Carrot Cake Overnight Oats
- Frittata with Bell Peppers
- Fruit and Nut Energy Bars
- Maple Oatmeal with Pecans
- Breakfast Casserole with Sausage
- Honey Nut Granola with Yogurt
- Savory Crepes with Spinach
- Cacao Banana Smoothie
- Baked Egg in Avocado
- Peach and Almond Overnight Oats
- Hash Brown Casserole with Cheese

Fluffy Buttermilk Pancakes
Ingredients:

- 1 cup all-purpose flour
- 2 tablespoons sugar
- 2 teaspoons baking powder
- 1/2 teaspoon baking soda
- 1/4 teaspoon salt
- 1 cup buttermilk
- 1 large egg
- 2 tablespoons melted butter
- Cooking spray or additional butter for the pan

Instructions:

1. **Mix Dry Ingredients:** In a bowl, whisk together flour, sugar, baking powder, baking soda, and salt.
2. **Combine Wet Ingredients:** In another bowl, combine buttermilk, egg, and melted butter.
3. **Combine Mixtures:** Pour the wet ingredients into the dry ingredients and stir until just combined; a few lumps are okay.
4. **Cook Pancakes:** Heat a non-stick skillet over medium heat and grease with cooking spray or butter. Pour 1/4 cup of batter for each pancake. Cook until bubbles form on the surface, then flip and cook until golden brown.
5. **Serve:** Serve warm with syrup or toppings of your choice.

Croissant Sandwich with Ham and Cheese

Ingredients:

- 2 large croissants
- 4 slices of ham
- 4 slices of cheese (Swiss or cheddar)
- 1 tablespoon Dijon mustard (optional)
- Fresh arugula or spinach (optional)

Instructions:

1. **Preheat Oven:** Preheat the oven to 350°F (175°C).
2. **Assemble Sandwich:** Slice the croissants in half. Spread Dijon mustard on the inside (if using), then layer with ham, cheese, and arugula.
3. **Bake:** Place the assembled sandwiches on a baking sheet and bake for 10-12 minutes, until the cheese is melted and the croissants are warmed.
4. **Serve:** Serve immediately.

Overnight Oats with Almond Milk

Ingredients:

- 1/2 cup rolled oats
- 1 cup almond milk
- 1 tablespoon chia seeds
- 1 tablespoon maple syrup or honey
- Fresh fruit and nuts for topping

Instructions:

1. **Combine Ingredients:** In a mason jar or bowl, combine rolled oats, almond milk, chia seeds, and maple syrup. Stir well.
2. **Refrigerate:** Cover and refrigerate overnight (or at least 4 hours).
3. **Serve:** In the morning, give the oats a good stir and top with fresh fruit and nuts before enjoying.

Mini Quiches with Spinach and Cheese
Ingredients:

- 6 large eggs
- 1 cup milk
- 1 cup fresh spinach (chopped)
- 1 cup shredded cheese (cheddar or mozzarella)
- 1/2 teaspoon salt
- 1/4 teaspoon pepper
- 1/2 teaspoon garlic powder (optional)
- Cooking spray or oil for greasing

Instructions:

1. **Preheat Oven:** Preheat the oven to 375°F (190°C) and grease a muffin tin.
2. **Mix Ingredients:** In a bowl, whisk together eggs, milk, salt, pepper, and garlic powder. Stir in spinach and cheese.
3. **Fill Muffin Tin:** Pour the mixture evenly into the greased muffin cups, filling each about 3/4 full.
4. **Bake:** Bake for 20-25 minutes, or until the quiches are set and lightly golden.
5. **Serve:** Allow to cool slightly before removing from the tin. Serve warm.

French Toast Sticks with Maple Syrup
Ingredients:

- 4 slices of bread (thick-cut, such as brioche or challah)
- 2 large eggs
- 1/2 cup milk
- 1 teaspoon vanilla extract
- 1/2 teaspoon cinnamon
- Cooking spray or butter for frying
- Maple syrup for serving

Instructions:

1. **Prepare Mixture:** In a shallow dish, whisk together eggs, milk, vanilla, and cinnamon.
2. **Cut Bread:** Cut each slice of bread into thirds to create sticks.
3. **Dip and Cook:** Dip each stick into the egg mixture, allowing excess to drip off. Heat a skillet over medium heat and grease with cooking spray or butter. Cook the sticks for 2-3 minutes on each side until golden brown.
4. **Serve:** Serve warm with maple syrup for dipping.

Smoothie Bowl with Granola
Ingredients:

- 1 banana (frozen)
- 1 cup mixed berries (frozen or fresh)
- 1/2 cup yogurt (Greek or regular)
- 1/2 cup almond milk (or milk of choice)
- Granola and fresh fruit for topping

Instructions:

1. **Blend Smoothie:** In a blender, combine the banana, mixed berries, yogurt, and almond milk. Blend until smooth.
2. **Pour into Bowl:** Pour the smoothie mixture into a bowl.
3. **Add Toppings:** Top with granola and fresh fruit as desired.
4. **Serve:** Enjoy immediately with a spoon.

Scones with Clotted Cream and Jam

Ingredients:

- 2 cups all-purpose flour
- 1 tablespoon baking powder
- 1/4 teaspoon salt
- 1/4 cup unsalted butter (cold, cubed)
- 1/4 cup sugar
- 3/4 cup heavy cream
- Clotted cream and jam for serving

Instructions:

1. **Preheat Oven:** Preheat the oven to 400°F (200°C) and line a baking sheet with parchment paper.
2. **Mix Dry Ingredients:** In a bowl, combine flour, baking powder, salt, and sugar.
3. **Cut in Butter:** Add the cold butter and mix until the mixture resembles coarse crumbs.
4. **Add Cream:** Pour in the heavy cream and stir until just combined. Turn the dough onto a floured surface and knead gently.
5. **Shape and Cut:** Pat the dough into a circle about 1 inch thick and cut into wedges. Place on the baking sheet.
6. **Bake:** Bake for 15-20 minutes or until golden brown.
7. **Serve:** Serve warm with clotted cream and jam.

Avocado Toast with Radish
Ingredients:

- 1 ripe avocado
- 2 slices of whole grain bread
- 1-2 radishes (thinly sliced)
- Lemon juice
- Salt and pepper to taste
- Optional: red pepper flakes or sesame seeds

Instructions:

1. **Toast Bread:** Toast the slices of bread until golden brown.
2. **Prepare Avocado:** In a bowl, mash the avocado with a fork and add a squeeze of lemon juice, salt, and pepper.
3. **Assemble Toast:** Spread the mashed avocado evenly on the toasted bread.
4. **Top with Radish:** Arrange the radish slices on top and sprinkle with additional seasoning if desired.
5. **Serve:** Enjoy immediately.

Chocolate Chip Banana Bread
Ingredients:

- 3 ripe bananas (mashed)
- 1/3 cup melted butter
- 1 teaspoon baking soda
- Pinch of salt
- 3/4 cup sugar
- 1 large egg (beaten)
- 1 teaspoon vanilla extract
- 1 cup all-purpose flour
- 1/2 cup chocolate chips

Instructions:

1. **Preheat Oven:** Preheat the oven to 350°F (175°C) and grease a 9x5-inch loaf pan.
2. **Combine Ingredients:** In a mixing bowl, mix mashed bananas with melted butter. Stir in baking soda and salt.
3. **Add Sugar:** Mix in the sugar, beaten egg, and vanilla.
4. **Add Flour and Chips:** Stir in the flour until just combined, then fold in chocolate chips.
5. **Bake:** Pour the batter into the prepared loaf pan and bake for 60-65 minutes or until a toothpick comes out clean.
6. **Cool and Serve:** Let cool in the pan for 10 minutes, then transfer to a wire rack to cool completely.

Poached Eggs on Toast
Ingredients:

- 2 large eggs
- 2 slices of bread (your choice)
- 1 tablespoon white vinegar (optional)
- Salt and pepper to taste
- Optional: fresh herbs for garnish

Instructions:

1. **Prepare Toast:** Toast the slices of bread to your liking.
2. **Poach Eggs:** Fill a saucepan with water and bring to a gentle simmer. Add vinegar (if using). Crack each egg into a small bowl, then gently slide into the water. Cook for about 3-4 minutes or until the whites are set.
3. **Remove Eggs:** Use a slotted spoon to remove the eggs and drain on a paper towel.
4. **Assemble:** Place the poached eggs on top of the toasted bread. Season with salt, pepper, and fresh herbs if desired.
5. **Serve:** Enjoy immediately.

Yogurt Parfait with Berries

Ingredients:

- 1 cup Greek yogurt
- 1 cup mixed berries (strawberries, blueberries, raspberries)
- 1/4 cup granola
- Honey or maple syrup (optional)

Instructions:

1. **Layer Ingredients:** In a glass or bowl, layer half of the yogurt, followed by half of the berries, and half of the granola.
2. **Repeat Layers:** Repeat the layers with the remaining yogurt, berries, and granola.
3. **Drizzle:** Drizzle with honey or maple syrup if desired.
4. **Serve:** Enjoy immediately.

Breakfast Burrito with Avocado

Ingredients:

- 2 large eggs
- 1/2 avocado (sliced)
- 1/4 cup shredded cheese (cheddar or your choice)
- 1 small tortilla
- Salsa (optional)
- Salt and pepper to taste

Instructions:

1. **Scramble Eggs:** In a skillet, scramble the eggs over medium heat until cooked through. Season with salt and pepper.
2. **Warm Tortilla:** Warm the tortilla in another skillet or microwave.
3. **Assemble Burrito:** Layer the scrambled eggs, avocado slices, and cheese on the tortilla.
4. **Roll Burrito:** Roll up the tortilla tightly, folding in the sides as you go.
5. **Serve:** Serve with salsa if desired.

Cinnamon Roll Pancakes
Ingredients:

- 1 cup all-purpose flour
- 2 tablespoons sugar
- 1 teaspoon baking powder
- 1/2 teaspoon baking soda
- 1/4 teaspoon salt
- 1 cup buttermilk
- 1 large egg
- 2 tablespoons melted butter
- 1/4 cup brown sugar
- 1 teaspoon cinnamon
- Optional: icing for drizzling

Instructions:

1. **Mix Dry Ingredients:** In a bowl, whisk together flour, sugar, baking powder, baking soda, and salt.
2. **Combine Wet Ingredients:** In another bowl, combine buttermilk, egg, and melted butter.
3. **Combine Mixtures:** Pour wet ingredients into dry ingredients and mix until just combined.
4. **Make Cinnamon Filling:** In a small bowl, mix brown sugar and cinnamon.
5. **Cook Pancakes:** Heat a skillet over medium heat. Pour 1/4 cup of batter onto the skillet. Before flipping, drizzle a bit of the cinnamon filling in a swirl pattern on top. Flip the pancake and cook until golden brown on both sides.
6. **Serve:** Serve warm with icing drizzled on top if desired.

Savory Breakfast Bowl with Quinoa
Ingredients:

- 1 cup cooked quinoa
- 2 large eggs (poached or fried)
- 1/2 avocado (sliced)
- 1/2 cup cherry tomatoes (halved)
- 1/4 cup feta cheese (crumbled)
- Olive oil
- Salt and pepper to taste
- Fresh herbs (parsley or cilantro)

Instructions:

1. **Prepare Quinoa:** In a bowl, add the cooked quinoa as the base.
2. **Add Eggs:** Top with the poached or fried eggs.
3. **Add Toppings:** Arrange avocado slices, cherry tomatoes, and crumbled feta on top.
4. **Drizzle and Season:** Drizzle with olive oil and season with salt, pepper, and fresh herbs.
5. **Serve:** Enjoy immediately.

Berry Smoothie with Oats

Ingredients:

- 1 cup mixed berries (fresh or frozen)
- 1/2 banana
- 1/2 cup Greek yogurt
- 1/2 cup almond milk (or milk of choice)
- 1/4 cup rolled oats
- 1 tablespoon honey or maple syrup (optional)

Instructions:

1. **Blend Ingredients:** In a blender, combine the mixed berries, banana, Greek yogurt, almond milk, rolled oats, and sweetener if using.
2. **Blend Until Smooth:** Blend until smooth and creamy.
3. **Serve:** Pour into a glass and enjoy immediately.

Omelette with Fresh Herbs
Ingredients:

- 3 large eggs
- 1 tablespoon milk
- Salt and pepper to taste
- 1/4 cup mixed fresh herbs (parsley, chives, basil)
- 1/4 cup cheese (cheddar or feta, optional)
- 1 tablespoon butter or olive oil

Instructions:

1. **Whisk Eggs:** In a bowl, whisk together the eggs, milk, salt, and pepper.
2. **Heat Pan:** In a skillet, heat butter or olive oil over medium heat.
3. **Cook Eggs:** Pour in the egg mixture and cook until edges start to set.
4. **Add Herbs and Cheese:** Sprinkle fresh herbs and cheese on one half of the omelette.
5. **Fold and Cook:** Fold the other half over and cook until fully set.
6. **Serve:** Slide onto a plate and enjoy.

Breakfast Tacos with Scrambled Eggs
Ingredients:

- 4 small corn or flour tortillas
- 4 large eggs
- 1/4 cup milk
- 1/2 cup cheese (cheddar or pepper jack)
- 1/2 avocado (sliced)
- Salsa or hot sauce
- Salt and pepper to taste

Instructions:

1. **Scramble Eggs:** In a bowl, whisk eggs, milk, salt, and pepper. In a skillet, scramble the egg mixture until cooked through.
2. **Warm Tortillas:** Warm the tortillas in another skillet or microwave.
3. **Assemble Tacos:** Divide scrambled eggs among tortillas and top with cheese, avocado slices, and salsa.
4. **Serve:** Enjoy immediately.

Granola with Yogurt and Honey
Ingredients:

- 1 cup granola
- 1 cup Greek yogurt
- 1 tablespoon honey
- Fresh fruit (berries or banana slices)

Instructions:

1. **Layer Ingredients:** In a bowl or glass, layer Greek yogurt, granola, and fresh fruit.
2. **Drizzle Honey:** Drizzle honey on top.
3. **Serve:** Enjoy immediately.

Sautéed Apples with Cinnamon
Ingredients:

- 2 apples (sliced)
- 1 tablespoon butter
- 1 tablespoon brown sugar
- 1 teaspoon cinnamon
- Optional: chopped nuts for topping

Instructions:

1. **Melt Butter:** In a skillet, melt the butter over medium heat.
2. **Sauté Apples:** Add sliced apples, brown sugar, and cinnamon. Sauté until apples are tender and caramelized, about 5-7 minutes.
3. **Serve:** Serve warm, topped with chopped nuts if desired.

Biscuit and Gravy Casserole
Ingredients:

- 1 can refrigerated biscuits
- 1 pound sausage (breakfast or Italian)
- 2 cups milk
- 1/4 cup flour
- Salt and pepper to taste
- Optional: shredded cheese

Instructions:

1. **Preheat Oven:** Preheat the oven to 350°F (175°C).
2. **Cook Sausage:** In a skillet, cook sausage over medium heat until browned. Remove from skillet and set aside.
3. **Make Gravy:** In the same skillet, add flour and cook for 1 minute. Gradually whisk in milk, stirring until thickened. Season with salt and pepper.
4. **Assemble Casserole:** In a baking dish, cut biscuits into quarters and layer on the bottom. Add sausage, then pour gravy over the top.
5. **Bake:** Bake for 25-30 minutes until biscuits are golden brown.
6. **Serve:** Serve warm, optionally topped with shredded cheese.

Chia Seed Pudding with Coconut
Ingredients:

- 1/2 cup chia seeds
- 2 cups coconut milk
- 1 tablespoon honey or maple syrup
- 1 teaspoon vanilla extract
- Fresh fruit for topping (mango, berries, etc.)

Instructions:

1. **Mix Ingredients:** In a bowl, combine chia seeds, coconut milk, honey, and vanilla extract.
2. **Refrigerate:** Stir well and refrigerate for at least 4 hours or overnight until it thickens.
3. **Serve:** Serve chilled, topped with fresh fruit.

Fruit Salad with Mint
Ingredients:

- 2 cups mixed fresh fruits (berries, melon, pineapple, etc.)
- 2 tablespoons fresh mint (chopped)
- 1 tablespoon honey (optional)
- Juice of 1 lime

Instructions:

1. **Combine Ingredients:** In a large bowl, mix together the fresh fruits, mint, honey (if using), and lime juice.
2. **Serve:** Serve immediately or chill for 30 minutes before serving.

Egg and Cheese Breakfast Muffin

Ingredients:

- 1 English muffin (split and toasted)
- 1 large egg
- 1 slice cheese (cheddar, American, etc.)
- Salt and pepper to taste
- Optional: sliced avocado or bacon

Instructions:

1. **Cook Egg:** In a small skillet, cook the egg to your liking (fried, scrambled, or poached).
2. **Assemble Muffin:** Place the cooked egg on one half of the toasted muffin, top with cheese, and season with salt and pepper.
3. **Serve:** Top with the other muffin half or any additional toppings and enjoy.

Coconut French Toast

Ingredients:

- 4 slices of bread
- 2 eggs
- 1/2 cup coconut milk
- 1 teaspoon vanilla extract
- 1/4 cup shredded coconut (for topping)
- Maple syrup for serving

Instructions:

1. **Prepare Mixture:** In a shallow dish, whisk together eggs, coconut milk, and vanilla extract.
2. **Dip Bread:** Dip each slice of bread into the mixture, allowing it to soak for a few seconds on each side.
3. **Cook:** In a skillet, cook the soaked bread over medium heat until golden brown on both sides.
4. **Serve:** Top with shredded coconut and serve with maple syrup.

Zucchini Bread with Walnuts

Ingredients:

- 1 1/2 cups grated zucchini
- 1 cup all-purpose flour
- 1/2 cup sugar
- 1/2 cup walnuts (chopped)
- 1/2 cup vegetable oil
- 2 eggs
- 1 teaspoon baking soda
- 1 teaspoon cinnamon
- 1/2 teaspoon salt

Instructions:

1. **Preheat Oven:** Preheat the oven to 350°F (175°C) and grease a loaf pan.
2. **Mix Ingredients:** In a bowl, combine grated zucchini, flour, sugar, walnuts, oil, eggs, baking soda, cinnamon, and salt.
3. **Pour and Bake:** Pour the mixture into the prepared loaf pan and bake for 50-60 minutes or until a toothpick comes out clean.
4. **Cool and Serve:** Let it cool before slicing and serving.

Lemon Ricotta Pancakes
Ingredients:

- 1 cup ricotta cheese
- 1/2 cup milk
- 2 large eggs
- Zest of 1 lemon
- 1 cup all-purpose flour
- 2 tablespoons sugar
- 2 teaspoons baking powder
- Butter for cooking

Instructions:

1. **Mix Wet Ingredients:** In a bowl, whisk together ricotta, milk, eggs, and lemon zest.
2. **Combine Dry Ingredients:** In another bowl, mix flour, sugar, and baking powder.
3. **Combine Both:** Fold the dry ingredients into the wet mixture until just combined.
4. **Cook Pancakes:** In a skillet, melt butter and cook pancakes until golden brown on both sides.
5. **Serve:** Serve warm with syrup or fresh fruit.

Tofu Scramble with Veggies

Ingredients:

- 1 block firm tofu (crumbled)
- 1 cup mixed vegetables (bell peppers, spinach, onions, etc.)
- 1 tablespoon olive oil
- 1 teaspoon turmeric
- Salt and pepper to taste
- Optional: nutritional yeast for flavor

Instructions:

1. **Sauté Vegetables:** In a skillet, heat olive oil and sauté mixed vegetables until tender.
2. **Add Tofu and Season:** Add crumbled tofu, turmeric, salt, and pepper. Cook for 5-7 minutes, stirring occasionally.
3. **Serve:** Optional: sprinkle with nutritional yeast before serving. Enjoy warm.

Bagel with Cream Cheese and Smoked Salmon
Ingredients:

- 1 bagel (your choice)
- 2 tablespoons cream cheese
- 4 oz smoked salmon
- Capers (optional)
- Fresh dill (optional)

Instructions:

1. **Toast Bagel:** Slice the bagel in half and toast until golden brown.
2. **Spread Cream Cheese:** Spread cream cheese evenly on each half of the bagel.
3. **Add Salmon:** Layer smoked salmon on top.
4. **Garnish:** Top with capers and fresh dill if desired. Serve immediately.

Raspberry Almond Overnight Oats
Ingredients:

- 1/2 cup rolled oats
- 1 cup almond milk
- 1/2 cup raspberries (fresh or frozen)
- 1 tablespoon almond butter
- 1 tablespoon honey or maple syrup (optional)
- Sliced almonds for topping

Instructions:

1. **Combine Ingredients:** In a jar or bowl, mix oats, almond milk, raspberries, almond butter, and sweetener if using.
2. **Refrigerate:** Cover and refrigerate overnight.
3. **Serve:** In the morning, stir and top with sliced almonds before serving.

Breakfast Flatbread with Eggs
Ingredients:

- 2 flatbreads or tortillas
- 4 large eggs
- 1/2 cup spinach (or other greens)
- 1/4 cup feta cheese (crumbled)
- Salt and pepper to taste
- Olive oil for cooking

Instructions:

1. **Cook Eggs:** In a skillet, heat olive oil and scramble eggs until just set. Add spinach and cook until wilted. Season with salt and pepper.
2. **Assemble Flatbreads:** On each flatbread, layer the scrambled eggs and spinach, then sprinkle with feta cheese.
3. **Serve:** Roll up and serve warm.

Sweet Potato Hash with Eggs
Ingredients:

- 2 medium sweet potatoes (diced)
- 1 red bell pepper (diced)
- 1 small onion (diced)
- 4 large eggs
- Olive oil for cooking
- Salt and pepper to taste
- Fresh herbs for garnish (optional)

Instructions:

1. **Sauté Vegetables:** In a skillet, heat olive oil and add sweet potatoes, bell pepper, and onion. Cook until sweet potatoes are tender, about 10-15 minutes.
2. **Add Eggs:** Create wells in the hash and crack an egg into each well. Cover and cook until eggs are set to your liking. Season with salt and pepper.
3. **Serve:** Garnish with fresh herbs if desired.

Porridge with Dried Fruits
Ingredients:

- 1 cup rolled oats
- 2 cups water or milk
- 1/2 cup mixed dried fruits (raisins, apricots, cranberries)
- 1 tablespoon honey or maple syrup (optional)
- Nuts or seeds for topping (optional)

Instructions:

1. **Cook Oats:** In a saucepan, bring water or milk to a boil. Add oats and dried fruits. Reduce heat and simmer for 5-7 minutes, stirring occasionally.
2. **Sweeten:** Stir in honey or maple syrup if desired.
3. **Serve:** Top with nuts or seeds before serving.

Blueberry Muffins
Ingredients:

- 1 cup all-purpose flour
- 1/2 cup sugar
- 1/2 cup milk
- 1/4 cup vegetable oil
- 1 large egg
- 1 teaspoon baking powder
- 1/2 teaspoon baking soda
- 1 cup fresh or frozen blueberries

Instructions:

1. **Preheat Oven:** Preheat the oven to 375°F (190°C) and line a muffin tin with paper liners.
2. **Mix Ingredients:** In a bowl, combine flour, sugar, baking powder, and baking soda. In another bowl, whisk together milk, oil, and egg. Combine wet and dry ingredients, then gently fold in blueberries.
3. **Bake:** Fill muffin cups about 2/3 full and bake for 18-20 minutes or until a toothpick comes out clean.
4. **Cool and Serve:** Let cool before serving.

Baked Apples with Oats
Ingredients:

- 4 medium apples (cored)
- 1 cup rolled oats
- 1/4 cup brown sugar
- 1 teaspoon cinnamon
- 1/4 cup butter (melted)
- 1/4 cup chopped nuts (optional)

Instructions:

1. **Preheat Oven:** Preheat the oven to 350°F (175°C).
2. **Prepare Filling:** In a bowl, mix oats, brown sugar, cinnamon, melted butter, and nuts if using.
3. **Stuff Apples:** Stuff each apple with the oat mixture and place in a baking dish.
4. **Bake:** Add a little water to the bottom of the dish and bake for 25-30 minutes until apples are tender.
5. **Serve:** Serve warm as a delicious breakfast or dessert.

Spinach and Feta Breakfast Wrap
Ingredients:

- 1 whole wheat tortilla
- 2 large eggs
- 1 cup fresh spinach
- 1/4 cup feta cheese (crumbled)
- Salt and pepper to taste
- Olive oil for cooking

Instructions:

1. **Sauté Spinach:** In a skillet, heat a little olive oil and sauté the spinach until wilted.
2. **Cook Eggs:** In a bowl, whisk the eggs and season with salt and pepper. Add to the skillet and scramble with the spinach.
3. **Assemble Wrap:** Place the egg and spinach mixture onto the tortilla, sprinkle with feta cheese, and roll it up. Serve warm.

Chocolate Smoothie with Peanut Butter
Ingredients:

- 1 banana (frozen or fresh)
- 1 tablespoon cocoa powder
- 1 tablespoon peanut butter
- 1 cup almond milk (or milk of choice)
- Ice cubes (optional)

Instructions:

1. **Blend Ingredients:** In a blender, combine the banana, cocoa powder, peanut butter, and almond milk. Add ice if desired.
2. **Blend Until Smooth:** Blend until smooth and creamy.
3. **Serve:** Pour into a glass and enjoy immediately.

Stuffed French Toast with Berries
Ingredients:

- 4 slices of bread (your choice)
- 1/2 cup cream cheese
- 1/2 cup mixed berries (fresh or frozen)
- 2 large eggs
- 1/2 cup milk
- 1 teaspoon vanilla extract
- Maple syrup for serving

Instructions:

1. **Prepare Filling:** In a bowl, mix cream cheese and berries together until combined.
2. **Stuff Bread:** Spread the cream cheese mixture between two slices of bread to make a sandwich.
3. **Mix Egg Mixture:** In another bowl, whisk together eggs, milk, and vanilla.
4. **Cook French Toast:** Dip each stuffed sandwich into the egg mixture, then cook in a skillet over medium heat until golden brown on both sides.
5. **Serve:** Serve warm with maple syrup.

Egg Salad on Toast
Ingredients:

- 4 hard-boiled eggs (chopped)
- 2 tablespoons mayonnaise
- 1 teaspoon Dijon mustard
- Salt and pepper to taste
- Whole grain bread for toasting

Instructions:

1. **Make Egg Salad:** In a bowl, combine chopped eggs, mayonnaise, Dijon mustard, salt, and pepper. Mix until well combined.
2. **Toast Bread:** Toast slices of whole grain bread.
3. **Serve:** Spread the egg salad on top of the toast and enjoy.

Avocado and Egg Breakfast Bowl
Ingredients:

- 1 ripe avocado (halved and pitted)
- 2 large eggs
- Salt and pepper to taste
- Red pepper flakes (optional)
- Fresh herbs for garnish (optional)

Instructions:

1. **Cook Eggs:** Poach or fry the eggs to your liking.
2. **Prepare Bowl:** In a bowl, place the avocado halves and season with salt, pepper, and red pepper flakes if desired.
3. **Add Eggs:** Top each avocado half with a cooked egg. Garnish with fresh herbs if desired and serve immediately.

Carrot Cake Overnight Oats
Ingredients:

- 1/2 cup rolled oats
- 1 cup almond milk
- 1/2 cup grated carrots
- 1 tablespoon maple syrup
- 1/2 teaspoon cinnamon
- 1 tablespoon chopped walnuts (optional)

Instructions:

1. **Combine Ingredients:** In a jar or bowl, mix oats, almond milk, grated carrots, maple syrup, and cinnamon.
2. **Refrigerate:** Cover and refrigerate overnight.
3. **Serve:** In the morning, stir and top with chopped walnuts before serving.

Frittata with Bell Peppers
Ingredients:

- 6 large eggs
- 1 cup bell peppers (diced)
- 1/2 cup onion (diced)
- Salt and pepper to taste
- Olive oil for cooking
- Fresh herbs for garnish (optional)

Instructions:

1. **Preheat Oven:** Preheat your oven to 350°F (175°C).
2. **Sauté Vegetables:** In a skillet, heat olive oil and sauté the onions and bell peppers until tender.
3. **Mix Eggs:** In a bowl, whisk together the eggs, salt, and pepper. Pour over the vegetables in the skillet.
4. **Cook and Bake:** Cook on the stove for a few minutes until the edges set, then transfer to the oven and bake for 15-20 minutes until fully set.
5. **Serve:** Let cool slightly, slice, and garnish with fresh herbs if desired.

Fruit and Nut Energy Bars
Ingredients:

- 1 cup mixed nuts (chopped)
- 1 cup dried fruits (such as dates, apricots, or raisins)
- 1/2 cup rolled oats
- 1/4 cup honey or maple syrup
- 1/2 teaspoon vanilla extract
- Pinch of salt

Instructions:

1. **Mix Ingredients:** In a bowl, combine chopped nuts, dried fruits, rolled oats, honey, vanilla extract, and salt. Mix well.
2. **Press Mixture:** Line a baking dish with parchment paper and press the mixture evenly into the bottom.
3. **Chill and Cut:** Refrigerate for at least an hour, then cut into bars.
4. **Store:** Store in an airtight container in the refrigerator for a quick snack or breakfast option.

Maple Oatmeal with Pecans
Ingredients:

- 1 cup rolled oats
- 2 cups water or milk
- 1/4 cup maple syrup
- 1/2 cup pecans (chopped)
- Pinch of salt
- Fresh fruit for topping (optional)

Instructions:

1. **Cook Oats:** In a saucepan, combine oats, water or milk, and a pinch of salt. Bring to a boil, then reduce heat and simmer for about 5 minutes, stirring occasionally.
2. **Add Maple Syrup:** Once the oats are cooked to your desired consistency, stir in the maple syrup and chopped pecans.
3. **Serve:** Divide into bowls and top with fresh fruit if desired.

Breakfast Casserole with Sausage
Ingredients:

- 6 large eggs
- 1 cup milk
- 1 pound breakfast sausage (cooked and crumbled)
- 2 cups diced bread (preferably stale)
- 1 cup shredded cheese (cheddar or your choice)
- Salt and pepper to taste

Instructions:

1. **Preheat Oven:** Preheat your oven to 350°F (175°C).
2. **Mix Ingredients:** In a large bowl, whisk together eggs, milk, salt, and pepper. Add the cooked sausage, diced bread, and cheese, mixing until combined.
3. **Bake:** Pour the mixture into a greased baking dish and bake for 30-35 minutes, or until set and golden on top.
4. **Serve:** Let cool slightly before cutting into squares to serve.

Honey Nut Granola with Yogurt
Ingredients:

- 2 cups rolled oats
- 1/2 cup nuts (such as almonds or walnuts)
- 1/2 cup honey
- 1/4 cup coconut oil (melted)
- 1/2 teaspoon cinnamon
- Yogurt for serving
- Fresh fruit for topping (optional)

Instructions:

1. **Preheat Oven:** Preheat your oven to 350°F (175°C).
2. **Mix Granola:** In a bowl, combine oats, nuts, honey, melted coconut oil, and cinnamon. Mix well until evenly coated.
3. **Bake:** Spread the mixture onto a baking sheet and bake for 20-25 minutes, stirring halfway through until golden brown.
4. **Serve:** Let cool and serve with yogurt and fresh fruit if desired.

Savory Crepes with Spinach
Ingredients:

- 1 cup all-purpose flour
- 2 large eggs
- 1 1/2 cups milk
- 1 cup fresh spinach (chopped)
- 1/2 cup cheese (such as feta or goat cheese)
- Salt and pepper to taste
- Olive oil for cooking

Instructions:

1. **Make Batter:** In a bowl, whisk together flour, eggs, milk, salt, and pepper until smooth. Let rest for 30 minutes.
2. **Cook Crepes:** Heat a non-stick skillet with olive oil over medium heat. Pour a small amount of batter into the pan, swirling to coat evenly. Cook for 1-2 minutes on each side until lightly golden.
3. **Fill Crepes:** Once cooked, fill each crepe with chopped spinach and cheese. Fold or roll and serve warm.

Cacao Banana Smoothie
Ingredients:

- 1 ripe banana
- 1 tablespoon cacao powder
- 1 cup almond milk (or milk of choice)
- 1 tablespoon honey or maple syrup (optional)
- Ice cubes (optional)

Instructions:

1. **Blend Ingredients:** In a blender, combine the banana, cacao powder, almond milk, and honey or maple syrup. Add ice if desired.
2. **Blend Until Smooth:** Blend until smooth and creamy.
3. **Serve:** Pour into a glass and enjoy immediately.

Baked Egg in Avocado
Ingredients:

- 1 ripe avocado
- 2 large eggs
- Salt and pepper to taste
- Optional toppings: chopped herbs, hot sauce, crumbled bacon, or cheese

Instructions:

1. **Preheat Oven:** Preheat your oven to 425°F (220°C).
2. **Prepare Avocado:** Cut the avocado in half and remove the pit. If needed, scoop out a little extra flesh to create enough space for the egg.
3. **Bake Eggs:** Place the avocado halves in a baking dish. Carefully crack an egg into each half. Season with salt and pepper.
4. **Bake:** Bake in the oven for 15-20 minutes, or until the egg whites are set and yolks are cooked to your liking.
5. **Serve:** Top with your choice of toppings and enjoy warm.

Peach and Almond Overnight Oats
Ingredients:

- 1 cup rolled oats
- 1 cup almond milk (or milk of choice)
- 1 ripe peach (diced)
- 2 tablespoons almond butter
- 1 tablespoon honey or maple syrup (optional)
- 1/4 teaspoon cinnamon
- Chopped almonds for topping

Instructions:

1. **Mix Ingredients:** In a bowl or jar, combine rolled oats, almond milk, diced peach, almond butter, honey or maple syrup, and cinnamon. Stir well to combine.
2. **Refrigerate:** Cover and refrigerate overnight (or at least 4 hours).
3. **Serve:** In the morning, stir the oats and add a splash of almond milk if desired. Top with chopped almonds and additional peach slices if preferred.

Hash Brown Casserole with Cheese
Ingredients:

- 1 package (30 oz) frozen hash browns
- 2 cups shredded cheddar cheese
- 1 can (10.5 oz) cream of mushroom soup
- 1 cup sour cream
- 1 small onion (diced)
- Salt and pepper to taste
- Optional toppings: green onions, extra cheese

Instructions:

1. **Preheat Oven:** Preheat your oven to 350°F (175°C).
2. **Mix Ingredients:** In a large bowl, combine hash browns, 1 1/2 cups of cheddar cheese, cream of mushroom soup, sour cream, diced onion, salt, and pepper.
3. **Bake Casserole:** Spread the mixture into a greased 9x13-inch baking dish. Bake for 45-50 minutes until golden and bubbly.
4. **Add Toppings:** Remove from the oven, sprinkle with the remaining cheddar cheese, and return to the oven for an additional 5-10 minutes until cheese is melted.
5. **Serve:** Let cool slightly before serving, garnished with green onions if desired.

www.ingramcontent.com/pod-product-compliance
Lightning Source LLC
LaVergne TN
LVHW081332060526
838201LV00055B/2596